The Profitable Auto Detail Shop

How to Start and Run a Successful Auto Detailing Business

J. M. Cook

ISBN: 978-0-615-22687-3

Cover Design by Colette Shirey

Cook • Shirey
Publications

CONTENTS

Contents

Contents

CHAPTER 6

Contents

Preface

When I decided to open a detail shop in Sacramento I already had years of experience doing mobile detail and working for detail shops. I was confident in my skills as an auto detailer and ready to take the leap and go into business for myself. I wanted to do it with the lowest possible start-up costs and make the business profitable within the shortest possible timeframe. I didn't want to work for years paying off bank loans. I found a way and in this book I will share what I learned through my experience. Looking back at what made my shop successful, I came up with ten key ideas.

Ten Keys to the Profitable Auto Detail Shop

- Keep start-up costs to a minimum.
- Choose the right business structure.
- Choose a great location.
- Don't waste money on advertising that doesn't pay off.
- Find the right pricing for your market.
- Develop a streamlined detailing system.
- Do premium work for a premium price.
- Build your retail business.
- Become a "One Stop Shop" for your customers.
- Boost profits through up-selling.

In this book we will cover these ten keys and more. This book will be very helpful for anyone thinking about opening their own detail shop. There are also great ideas and information for people who already have a shop and are looking for ways to improve profitability. From out-sourcing and up-selling to step-by-step detailing systems, this book covers it all.

CHAPTER

Start-up Considerations

Estimate your Startup Costs

If you watch your budget and keep your overhead low, starting an auto detail business can be done with relatively little starting capitol compared to most auto related businesses. Your major startup costs will be for purchasing detailing equipment, office equipment and advertising. You can start small and build it up, or open additional locations once you are running smoothly. Below are some estimated costs to consider.

Shop Equipment

Pressure washer	$500
(2) High speed buffers	$500
Porter Cable orbital	$200
Gem orbital polisher (16 lbs)	$300
Carpet extractor	$1300
Air compressor	$500
(2) Wet-Dry vacs	$300
Detailing tools	$500
Detailing products	$500
Detail cart, and storage shelves	$600
(2) Tripod work lights	$100

>>> **Total: $5,300**

Office Equipment

Computer and Printer	$1000
Quickbooks Pro	$200
Fax machine	$100
Phone system	$300
Security system	$1000
Office supplies	$200
Office furniture	$600

>>> Total: $3,400

Advertising

Signage	$1000
Yellow Page Ad	$400 (monthly)
Brochures and business cards	$300
T-shirts	$500

>>> Total: $2,200

Other

Washer & Dryer	$800
Insurance	$200 (monthly)
Licenses	$100
Merchant services account	$200
Lease	$1200 (monthly)

>>>Total: $2,500

Grand Total: $13,400

In addition to the starting capitol required to get up and running, you should also have at least $10,000 in back-up funds for unforeseen expenses and for helping with operating expenses. Even including the $10,000 in back-up funds you are still looking at less than $25,000 for start-up costs!

Choose a Business Structure

One of the first decisions that you will have to make as a business owner is how your business should be structured. This decision will have long-term implications, so you may want to consult with an accountant and attorney to help you select the form of ownership that is right for you.

Sole Proprietorship

The sole proprietorship is a simple, informal structure that is inexpensive to form. Many small detail shops start out as sole proprietorships. These businesses are owned by one person, usually the individual who has day-to-day responsibilities for running the business. Sole proprietors own all the assets of the business and the profits generated by it. They also assume complete responsibility for any of its liabilities or debts. In the eyes of the law and the public, you are one in the same with the business.

Partnerships

In a Partnership, two or more people share ownership of a single business. If you have a good friend or a family member that you can trust, you might consider a partnership. You can also form a partnership with your spouse. Like proprietorships, the law does not distinguish between the business and its owners. It's a good idea to have a legal agreement that sets forth how decisions will be made, profits will be shared, disputes will be resolved, how future partners will be admitted to the partnership, how partners can be bought out, and what steps will be taken to dissolve the partnership when needed. They also must decide up-front how much time and capital each will contribute, etc.

General Partnership

General Partnership is the most common partnership you would form for an auto detail business. Partners divide responsibility for management and liability as well as the shares of profit or loss according to their internal agreement. Equal shares are assumed unless there is a written agreement that states differently.

Limited and Partnership with Limited Liability

Limited means that most of the partners have limited liability (to the extent of their investment) as well as limited input regarding management decisions, which generally encourages investors for short-term projects or for investing in capital assets. This form of ownership is not often used for operating retail or service businesses. Forming a limited partnership is more complex and formal than that of a general partnership.

Corporations

A corporation chartered by the state in which it is headquartered is considered by law to be a unique entity, separate and apart from those who own it. A corporation can be taxed, it can be sued, and it can enter into contractual agreements. The owners of a corporation are its shareholders.

Subchapter S Corporations

A tax election only; this election enables the shareholder to treat the earnings and profits as distributions and have them pass through directly to their personal tax return. The catch here is that the shareholder, if working for the company, and if there is a profit, must pay him/herself wages, and must meet standards of "reasonable compensation". This can vary by geographical region as well as occupation, but the basic rule is to pay yourself what you would have to pay someone to do your job, as long as there is enough profit. If you do not do this, the

IRS can reclassify all of the earnings and profit as wages, and you will be liable for all of the payroll taxes on the total amount.

Limited Liability Company (LLC)

The LLC is a relatively new type of hybrid business structure that is now permissible in most states. It is designed to provide the limited liability features of a corporation and the tax efficiencies and operational flexibility of a partnership. Formation is more complex and formal than that of a general partnership. The owners are members, and the duration of the LLC is usually determined when the organization papers are filed. The time limit can be continued, if desired, by a vote of the members at the time of expiration. LLCs must not have more than two of the four characteristics that define corporations: Limited liability to the extent of assets, continuity of life, centralization of management, and free transferability of ownership interests.

<u>Choose a Location</u>

This is one of the most important decisions you will make. It will affect your business and profitability for as long as you remain at that location. If you go to big you might be paying for space that isn't necessary. If you go too small you might outgrow the shop faster than planned. Look for a shop that has at least 1000 sq ft. of open space. This is enough room to work on two cars at a time and store up to four when needed. The space should have good overhead lighting and plenty of electrical outlets. A small office with a waiting area on the premises is a big plus.

Make sure the location is zoned to do auto detailing. Also, because of environmental laws regarding storm drainage systems, it is extremely important to look for a shop that has access to a wash bay for washing and de-greasing the cars. The drain must have a sand trap and oil separator and it must drain to the sewer system. If you can't find a location with an EPA compliant wash bay, there are car wash mats you can purchase. Another option is to run the cars down to a local self service car wash and de-grease the engine and do the initial wash there. Check with your local government municipal office or the EPA regional office in your area to see what you need to do to be compliant.

If you plan to do wholesale work for dealers, it's a good idea to look for a location near auto dealerships. This will cut down on driving time. If you can find a location next to a place that's offering paintless dent repair or bumper repair and painting that would be perfect.

Register your Business Name

When choosing a business name it is usually best to keep it short and simple. Using the words "Auto Detail" or "Auto Detailing" in the name is a good idea.

Sole proprietorships and partnerships have the option of choosing a fictitious business name, which typically must be registered. Corporations don't have to register DBAs in many states unless they do business under a name other than the one cited on their incorporation documents.

Find out what your state requires regarding registering a DBA, because registration rules vary among states. Many states just require that a registration fee be paid at the county clerk's office. However, some states require that a fictitious name notice be placed in a local newspaper as part of DBA registration.

Obtain your Business License

The only license you will likely need to open an auto detail business is a business license. You apply for this license at the licensing department of the city in which you are opening your shop. The cost is minimal but varies by state. Your business license must be renewed every year.

Business Checking and Merchant Services

Once you have your business license and your location address, you can open your business checking account. This is also a good time to set up your merchant services account for credit card processing.

Insurance

The one type of insurance you will definitely need is commercial garagekeeper's liability insurance. If you have employees, you will have to have workers' compensation insurance. Some other types of insurance you might want to consider are property insurance, business interruption insurance, disability insurance, bonding insurance and health insurance.

Commercial Garagekeeper's Liability Insurance

This is the most important insurance coverage you will need. You should have at least a $1 million policy. With this type of insurance you will be covered for any damage that may occur to a customer vehicle, whether in the shop or while driving. You will also be covered for any injuries to a customer that may occur in your shop.

Workers' Compensation Insurance

If you have one or more employees, workers' compensation is required by law. You must provide coverage for all full- and part-time employees or face federal and state penalties. Each state develops its own regulations to ensure that businesses provide compensation and health benefits to employees who are hurt or become ill on the job. Workers' compensation insurance is also a no-fault policy – your employees can usually receive benefits for a workplace injury even if you weren't directly responsible. In turn, the employee receives compensation but can't sue your company for negligence.

Advertising and Marketing

Tip: Don't buy advertising from every shmuck that comes in to your shop. I promise you will be throwing money away.

Yellow Page Ad

The most important and probably the only advertising you will need is an ad in your local ATT Yellow Pages. This and word of mouth will be your main sources of new customers. Since everyone gets that phonebook, you don't really need to bother with other phonebooks. Along with your Yellow Page ad, you will also get a basic listing on Yellowpages.com. We had a lot of customers who found us online this way. As soon as you know your location address, find out the deadline for getting your ad done. The book only comes out once a year and you don't want to miss it.

You should include the following in your ad:

- ✓ Your business name, phone number and address
- ✓ List the services you offer (Don't list prices.)
- ✓ Include the statement "Fully Licensed and Insured"
- ✓ Include the statement "Pick up and delivery available"
- ✓ Include the statement "Free Insurance Estimates"
- ✓ If you are a BBB member include their logo.

Join the Better Business Bureau

Joining the Better Business Bureau lends credibility to your business. Some people will only do business with BBB members. Put their logo on your advertising showing you are a member. http://welcome.bbb.org/

Business Cards and Flyers

Create a cool business card and a professional flyer or brochure. There is software that lets you do it yourself or you can go to a professional printer. When it's slow go out and introduce yourself to other local businesses and leave cards and flyers to promote your business.

Below is a list of some of the types of businesses who could be potential customers or may refer their customers to you. Can you think of others? Be creative.

- Limousine services
- Auto body shops
- Mechanic shops
- Specialty parts shops
- Real estate offices
- Automobile clubs

Gift Certificates

Offer gift certificates. These sell great around Fathers Day and Mothers Day. The great thing about this is you get paid right when they buy them. Be sure to individually number each gift certificate and keep a log.

T-Shirts

Create cool t-shirts with your business name and logo. It looks professional and they are comfortable to work in.

Signage

Your exterior signage is very important. It can help bring in a lot of new business and is usually a potential customer's first impression of your shop. You want a professional looking sign with the business name lettering as large as possible to be seen by street traffic. If the name of your business doesn't include the words "Auto Detail" or "Auto Detailing" you should think about including these words in your signage. It should be clear that the sign is for an auto detail shop. Stay away from fancy lettering that may be hard to read from a distance. Before ordering any signage you should check out the local ordinances. Also, some locations may have their own requirements regarding signage, so check on this before ordering your signs.

CHAPTER

Detailing Equipment, Tools and Products

Below is a basic shopping list of items that you will need to purchase for your detail shop before you open for business. Most of these supplies can be purchased from your local distributors. You should always use professional grade products. We recommend Car Brite (www.carbrite.com), PRO® (www.prowax.com) and 3M products (www.3M.com). If there is a distributor in your area they will come to your shop every week with their trucks loaded with detail goodies. We used their products on a daily basis and know that they work well. Also included on the list are some of the particular products we used and recommend.

3M products can be found at your local automotive paint supply store. Costco is a good place to purchase certain items like pressure washers and shop-vacs.

Detailing Equipment

- ☐ **Pressure Washer** - You will need a basic pressure washer to use in the wash bay for washing and de-greasing purposes. The Karcher 2600 psi model can be purchased at Costco. Their price is very reasonable, around $400, and if you ever have any problems with the unit, it can be returned.

☐ **High Speed Buffers -** Rotary buffers provide a more aggressive paint correction than is possible with orbital polishers. Rotary buffers rotate the head of the buffer through revolutions. These revolutions are circular and are called RPM's; revolutions per minute. Most quality high speed rotary buffers are variable speed meaning you can adjust the buffers speed anywhere from 0-3000 RPM's. Rotary buffers are usually used with compounds and polishes to remove imperfections like repairable light to medium scratches, swirls and paint oxidation. It's a good idea to have at least two buffers in case one ever needs repair. That way you are never without a buffer. The Dewalt Heavy Duty Variable Speed Buffer and the Makita Variable Speed Buffer are good buffers to consider. You will need the Velcro ® backing plate.

WARNING! Without proper training and practice it is possible to cause damage to painted surfaces with high speed rotary buffers.

☐ **Random Orbital -** The random orbital is a quick and efficient way to apply and remove wax and sealant. The Porter Cable #7424 is a good one to consider. You will need a Velcro ® backing plate and 6" finishing pads.

- **Gem Orbital Polisher (16lb) -** You might be able to get this from your local distributor. If not, it can be purchased online. This orbital works great for eliminating the swirl marks caused by high speed rotary buffers. Unlike the high speed buffer, the orbital "oscillates", or duplicates the motion of your hand as if you were hand waxing the surface of a car. The difference is that the Gem orbital creates 1700 oscillations per minute.

- **Carpet Extractor -** A carpet extractor will allow you to quickly and proficiently clean interior carpets and upholstery. A carpet extractor is made up of three main mechanical components; a powerful vacuum motor to "extract" the dirty water, a pressurized pump to inject the water into the carpet and upholstery fibers, and a heating system to provide hot water to break down the dirt and grime quickly. The extractor will also have a solution tank for the clean water to be held and a recovery tank which collects the dirty water.

- **Air Compressor -** The air compressor will mostly be used for blowing out and cleaning the nooks and crannies and hard to reach areas in a car. If you will be using the air compressor to power pneumatic tools you will need one that fulfills the CFM (cubic feet per minute) requirements of the equipment. Otherwise, a 20 – 28 gallon electric air compressor will probably be sufficient for your needs. The "oil-less" air compressors tend to be very loud when the pump is running. Choose one with an oil lubricated pump for quieter operation. Campbell Hausfeld makes a good selection of air compressors to choose from. The 26 gallon, VT6233 is one model to consider.

☐ **Wet-Dry Vac -** Choose a vacuum with at least a 5 hp motor and a 12 gallon tank.

Detailing Tools and Supplies

- ☐ Polishing pads
- ☐ Yellow foam waffle cutting pads (PRO®)
- ☐ White wool cutting pads
- ☐ Finishing pads (6") for Portal Cable orbital
- ☐ Bonnets for Gem orbital
- ☐ Wax applicators
- ☐ Spray bottles and squeeze bottles
- ☐ Wire brush for white walls
- ☐ Nylon brushes for scrubbing carpets
- ☐ Small soft detail brushes
- ☐ Razor blade scraper
- ☐ Single edge razor blades
- ☐ Chamois
- ☐ Wash mitts
- ☐ Bug sponge
- ☐ Terry cloth towels
- ☐ Micro-fiber towels
- ☐ Ultra fine steel wool #0000
- ☐ 2000 grit sand paper
- ☐ Heat Gun
- ☐ Foam pad cleaning tools
- ☐ Wool pad spur

Detailing Products

- ☐ Perfect-It lll Rubbing Compound (3M)
- ☐ Duz-All (PRO®)
- ☐ Yellow Carnauba Wax (PRO ®)
- ☐ Sleek (Car Brite) Great for dark colored cars!
- ☐ Polish (Car Brite or PRO ®)
- ☐ Paint Sealant (PRO ® Polymer ll)
- ☐ Detailing clay
- ☐ Exterior dressing (Car Brite Bumper Kote)
- ☐ Clear plastic cleaner and polish (3M)
- ☐ 303 Aerospace Protectant
- ☐ 303 High Tech Fabric Guard
- ☐ De-greaser
- ☐ Tire dressing
- ☐ Car wash soap (Cherry Bomb from Car Brite is a good choice)
- ☐ DX330 wax and tar remover (found at an automotive paint supply store)
- ☐ Wheel acid (Car Brite)
- ☐ Acid-free wheel cleaner
- ☐ Interior shampoo
- ☐ Carpet extractor solution
- ☐ Spot cleaner for carpets and upholstery

- ☐ Interior cleaner
- ☐ Leather cleaner and conditioner (Lexol)
- ☐ Fabric guard (PRO ®)
- ☐ Interior dressing (We recommend using a water based product so that you can also use it for dressing the engine.)

CHAPTER

Setting up Shop

<u>Shop Layout</u>

The layout of an auto detail shop is usually not very complicated. Most of the space will be used for working on the cars. Think about how you can use your space as efficiently as possible. Draw it out on paper and try different configurations. What is the best way to position the cars in the shop so that the doors can be opened all the way? How many cars can you realistically work on at one time in the shop? Is there a way to position the cars so that either one can be pulled out without having to move the other? You will probably have to actually pull cars into the shop to figure this out.

Check that the electrical outlets are conveniently located in the work space.

Check that the lighting in the works space is sufficient. If not, add additional lighting.

Install the air lines from the air compressor to the work area. Ideally they will be off the ground and conveniently located in the work space.

You will want plenty of shelving against the walls to store product and supplies.

If you will be installing a washer and dryer for cleaning your towels, you should locate them at the back of the shop. Otherwise, a good alternative is to have a towel service with a supply company like Cintas that delivers fresh towels weekly. If you have a towel service make sure they bring you towels to use only on the windows along with towels for detailing.

If you will be setting up a counter area for your computer and printer inside the shop, try to locate it close to the front so that your customers don't have to walk through the shop.

<u>Organizing the Shop</u>

Organizing the shop is very important. A clean and organized shop makes the best impression on your customers and makes for a pleasant and safe workplace. Being organized also saves you time. You don't want to waste your time running around in circles looking for your favorite polish.

Organize a wheeled cart with your favorite polish, wax, sealant, buffing pads and detailing tools. You can even hang the buffer on it. It's nice to have everything right there when you need it.

Organize your product and supplies on the shelves. This makes it much easier to keep track of what you need to order when the distributor truck comes by.

Keep a schedule for customer appointments. If you are picking up a vehicle make sure to note the address. It's always a good idea to give your customer a call the day before to confirm their appointment.

Put up a key rack for storing your customer's car keys. Train everyone in the shop to always hang the keys on the rack after the car is pulled into the shop. This helps to prevent the keys from getting locked in the car or going home with an employee.

Retail Service Orders

Have service orders printed for retail work. They should be triplicate forms. You will fill out this form after evaluating the car with the customer. The information from this form will later be entered into Quickbooks. When it has been nearly a year since a customer's last detail, you can mail them a friendly reminder to let them know that their car is due for detail

The following should be included on the service order.

- ✓ Service order number
- ✓ Your business name, address and phone number
- ✓ A section for the customer's contact information
- ✓ A section for the customer's vehicle information
- ✓ A checklist of all the retail services you offer
- ✓ A section for writing in prices
- ✓ A section for customer signature and date
- ✓ A Liability Disclaimer

Wholesale Log Sheet

Print up a log sheet for keeping track of your wholesale work. You can do this yourself with any word processor software. There is usually space on one sheet for 4 - 5 cars.

The following information should be included for each car.

- ✓ The date work was done
- ✓ Customer name
- ✓ The make, model, year and color of the vehicle

- ✓ VIN#
- ✓ stock#, if available
- ✓ Work performed
- ✓ Amount charged

This information can be put into Quickbooks so that you can print an invoice for each vehicle.

What to Track in Quickbooks

- ✓ Retail work
- ✓ Wholesale work
- ✓ Gift certificate sales
- ✓ Sub-contractor payments
- ✓ Vendor payments
- ✓ Employee payroll
- ✓ Business checking account (deposits / withdrawals).

Putting Together your Team

Employees

You may want to wait on hiring any employees until you absolutely need them. Besides paying employees wages there are the additional costs of payroll processing and workers compensation insurance.

When you do decide to take on employees, it's a good idea to do so on a trial basis so that you know they are going to be a good fit. The hardest thing we encountered running a detail shop was finding good hard working people who take pride in their work. If you can find someone who doesn't mind hard work and takes pride in doing a good job, you should hang on to that person.

Using Sub-Contractors

One of the best ways to make money in this business is up-selling additional services. Even if you don't know how to do those services, you can still offer them to your customers then outsource the work to local specialists. You want to be a "One Stop Shop" for your customers. To do this you will need to put together your team of "subs".

You are striving to be the best detailer in your town so your subs should also be the best at what they do! After all, you will be the one who has to answer to your customers if they are unhappy. It is also very important that they are dependable since you will usually need them to do the work during the same day that you sell the service.

How do you find good subs? Word of mouth usually works the best. Start asking around town. You can also find them in the phone book. They are usually business owners just like you who are specialists at their particular service. Always ask them for the "dealer rate" or "wholesale rate". Just remember everything is negotiable and they really want the work. Be sure to research the local retail rates for each of the services you want to offer at your shop so that you can negotiate the best wholesale rate.

Once you establish a relationship with a sub, you can start re-selling their services to your customers at a retail rate. After you make the sale to your customer, you just call up your sub and let them know that you have work for them. Usually the car will be in for a detail and you will have the whole day to get all the work done. Most services can be done at your shop so you don't have to drive your customer's car all over town. It's a win-win situation!

You should keep a record of all payments made to each sub in Quickbooks. At the end of the year you just mail them a 1099 form. Since they are sub-contractors, not employees, you will not have to worry about payroll or workers compensation insurance.

We outsourced all the different services listed below.

- Paintless dent repair
- Bumper repair
- Paint touch-up
- Windshield repair
- Window tinting
- Upholstery repair
- Convertible top repair or replacement.

Of all these services, paintless dent repair is a must have. If no one in your shop is trained to do PDR, find an experienced mobile PDR tech who will give you a good wholesale rate.

CHAPTER

Customer Service and Pricing

<u>Pricing Retail Work</u>

This is the work that you really want. You get to charge your full retail price and there is always the opportunity to make more money with additional services. To build your retail business you must put out quality work. This will generate repeat customers and customer referrals. It takes time to build a retail clientele but it will pay off in the long run.

One place to start when it comes to pricing your retail services is your competition. Call other local shops and find out what they are charging. But remember, the idea isn't to beat their price. The idea is to build your reputation as the best in town so that you can charge a premium price. Start at the high end of the scale and adjust your prices lower if necessary.

Below is a list of some services we offered in our shop in Sacramento, Ca with prices. We would adjust our prices higher for larger vehicles like SUV's and Pick-up trucks.

- Complete Detail $200 - $300
- Interior Detail $150
- Exterior Detail $150 - $200
- Wash and Wax $75

- Deluxe Wash $40
- New Car Protection Package $300

When the Phone Rings

Always answer with your business name. Be prepared to answer questions regarding pricing and the services you offer. Tell them everything you will do to their car. Write it down if you need to. Telling them everything step by step will usually get you the sale. Always be friendly, knowledgeable and professional.

When you are pricing a detail you should be estimating the amount of time the job will take and price accordingly. You can only do so much in a day so you need to get paid adequately for your time.

Asking the questions below will give you some important information on which to base your quote.

- ✓ **"What kind of car is it?"**
  This will tell you the size of the vehicle. Is it a small convertible with two doors? Or is it a larger vehicle like a Cadillac Escalade? Of course, a larger vehicle is more time consuming.

✓ **"What color?"**

Dark colored cars always take more time because it's at least a three step process. With a dark colored car always cut, polish and wax. Light colored cars usually take less time.

✓ **"What year?"**

The year is very important to know when pricing. The newer the car is, the less time it will likely take to detail. If the car is only two years old, it's usually still in good shape.

✓ **"When was the last time it was detailed?"**

It's good to know if the car gets detailed yearly or if it has never been detailed before. If the vehicle is 5 years old, never been detailed and is a dark color. You are going to spend all day on that one.

✓ **"Do you take it through the car wash?"**

Car washes use heavy duty detergents. They tend to dry out the finish which leads to heavy oxidation and scratches. That means a lot more time will be spent working on the exterior.

The actual price will depend on the condition of the car. Until you can actually see the car it's a good idea to quote a price range rather than a set price. If they are calling for an estimate for insurance work, always have them bring the car to you so that you can give an accurate price.

Evaluating the Car with your Customer

When the customer brings their car in for detail it's important whenever possible to evaluate the car with the customer present. One reason to do this is so that the customer will not mistakenly blame you for something that was previously damaged. Another reason to have the customer present is that it's the best opportunity to offer additional services and make more money.

Walk around the entire car with the customer and point out any existing damage or imperfections such as dents, dings, scratches, scuffs, chips, heavy oxidation or water spots. If the car is extremely dirty you will need to wash it before you can do a proper evaluation.

Once the evaluation is complete, you will finalize the pricing and write up the service order. Fill in the customer contact information, vehicle information and services to be performed.

Write in the prices and have the customer sign. If you have a triplicate form, give the customer a copy. Don't forget to get the customer's car keys.

If the customer is not present during the evaluation, just call and make them aware of any issues and offer any applicable services.

The following is a list of some of the things to look for during your evaluation.

Exterior
- Acid rain, water spots, fallout
- Heavy oxidation
- Medium to heavy scratches and scuffs
- Dings and dents
- Bumper scuffs
- Paint over-spray
- Excessive tree sap
- Excessive road grime
- Chipped paint
- Chipped or cracked windows
- Excessively dirty convertible top

Interior

- Condition of the seats
- Excessively dirty – carpets or mats
- Faded carpets
- Excessive pet hair
- Stains
- Condition of headliner
- Odors

It's also important to be there when the customer picks up their car. This is the most gratifying moment of this whole business. This is why I did this line of work for nearly 20 years. My customers were mostly blown away! They could not believe this was the same car they brought to me earlier. If you take pride in your work you will get the same response.

Boost Your Profits through Up-Selling

When we owned our detail shop in Sacramento, Ca. we often quoted the price of $250 for a complete detail over the phone. After up-selling scratch removal, dent repair or a paint sealant the total would be anywhere from $350 to $600. Our customers were very happy with their cars and we made more money than we would have if we only did a detail.

When you evaluate a car with the customer this is your best opportunity to up-sell all the services you offer and make more money. Though you may have already discussed their car on the phone, now you can really see what needs to be done. Never do a hard sale. Just point out issues and let them know that you can take care of it for them. You want to become a "one stop shop". Most of the time they are happy that it can all be done at one time and one place. They don't have to drive around town to different shops and they only have to do without their car for one day.

One of the most common services to sell is PDR work. Everyone gets door dings. Selling PDR is easy. Just point out any door dings and ask if they would like to have them repaired. PDR is usually charged by the dent or the panel. Check local dent repair businesses to get an idea of the retail pricing. Since the customer is already getting work done and is not shopping around for the lowest price, your pricing can be at the higher end of the scale.

Most PDR jobs require the technician to get behind the dent and massage the metal back into place using tools called dent rods. A good PDR technician can remove damage from the size of a dime to 2 or 3 inches in diameter. In many cases, after the repair is complete, there is little or no evidence that a dent ever existed. Some very experienced PDR techs can even repair basketball size dents. We used two different PDR techs. One was great at taking out the smaller dings. The other technician we used specialized in removing bigger sized dents and hail damage. It's great if you know someone who can do the bigger dents because you can charge your customers any where from $400 - $800 per dent. The customer will be happy because that is a fraction of what it would cost at a body shop and they don't want to go through their insurance because it might affect their premiums. So we charged the customer $400 - $800 and I would pay my tech $100. As you can see, outsourcing PDR has the potential to make a lot of extra money.

Bumper repair is another great way to make some extra cash. A lot of times rear and front bumpers get scratched up and even dented. Let your customer know that you can have their bumper repaired and re-painted. I would typically charge my customers $350 for this service. The painter I used was mobile and he would come to the shop and do the work. He would charge me $125 to repair and re-paint a bumper. Let your customer know that you will need to keep the car an extra day for this service. Always try to get the car painted before doing the detail because the painter might get overspray all over the car and you will need to remove it.

Another common service that you can offer to customers when they have their car in for a complete or exterior detail is a paint sealant application. This is sold as an upgrade to wax. We charged $100 to upgrade to a paint sealant.

The main difference between wax and sealant is that wax sits on top of the paint and lasts up to two months before breaking down from sun and weather, less time if they run their car through a car wash. Paint sealant actually bonds to the paint and lasts six months to one year. Once the sealant is applied you can apply a wax over the sealant for a glossier finish.

Below is a list of some of the additional services you can offer your customers.

- Water spot removal (acid wash)
- Overspray removal
- Oxidation removal
- Scratch removal (wet sanding)
- Swirl removal

- Paintless dent repair (PDR)
- Paint sealant application (Pro ® Polymer ll)
- Fabric guard application
- New car protection package
- Bumper repair
- Touch-up paint
- Upholstery repair
- Windshield repair
- Window tinting
- Plastic window reconditioning
- Convertible top protection
- Pinstriping
- Carpet and vinyl dyes (Car Brite and Pro ®)

You should become knowledgeable about any services you are outsourcing so that you can answer any questions your customers may have.

Pricing Wholesale Work

Wholesale work is generally work you do for auto dealerships. You are a sub-contractor and you will get a 1099 from each dealer you do work for at the end of the year. The reason you offer them a wholesale rate is that they keep steady work coming into the shop. But don't let your shop get overwhelmed by wholesale. It is the lowest paying work and you really want to build your retail business.

With wholesale work we would generally charge $100 per car for a complete detail. That sounds like a great deal but many dealerships want to pay even less than that. If detailers would come together and stop doing work for $50 a car, the pricing could go higher.

When you go to a major dealership to offer your services, always ask for the service manager. One way to get the account is to offer to do a detail on one of their cars for free. If they like what they see, go from there. You are going to have to show insurance papers to the larger dealerships. They want to make sure you are insured to drive their cars. If you do score a large account, make sure you have the man power to get all the cars done.

Once you start putting out quality work. Find a smaller used car dealer who only buys cleaner luxury cars. That's the gravy account you really want to be doing for wholesale. You can charge them anywhere from $100 - $250 a car because you can up-sell additional services to them. For instance, if the car just came back from the body shop and has over-spray all over it, call the customer up and ask if they want it removed. They will always want it removed, so charge them for it. Just remember that this account is bringing you a lot of work every week so you can't charge them retail prices, but you can charge for the extra stuff you're doing. Always stay in good terms with the dealers with the nicer cars. Their cars are much easier to clean up and take up less time out of your day.

How do you find these great accounts? You can look in the yellow pages or a lot of times they will find you because of word of mouth. They heard you were putting out great work and they want to take their cars to the best.

Key points to consider regarding wholesale accounts:
Make sure you charge a reasonable amount for your effort. Set your price and stick to it. If you do a great job, they will keep coming back to you. Be consistent.

Even though they pay a wholesale price, dealerships can be very demanding.

Keep good records of all the cars you do for dealers. Keep track of the stock numbers.

The larger dealerships pay only once a month. The smaller guys are more flexible. Always work out a pay program. For example: Tell them to pay you at the end of every week.

The bottom line is since dealers are paying a discounted rate you can't spend as much time as you would on a retail job. To make wholesale work profitable you have to find a way to cut down the time spent on their cars but still put out quality work so that your customers are happy.

CHAPTER

The Complete Detail

The Complete Detail (3 Way) includes the Engine Detail, Exterior Detail and Interior Detail. This is the most common service that customers and dealers will want.

Preparing For a Complete Detail

Pressure Wash the Floor Mats

When you do a Complete Detail or Interior Detail, you should pressure wash the mats. This is the best way to get them really clean.

Lay the mats out in the wash bay and spray them with degreaser, then scrub them with a nylon brush and soapy water. Use the pressure washer to force the soap and dirt out. Keep the tip of the wand about 3-4 inches from the mat. Start at the top of the mat and move the wand slowly from one side to the other, zigzagging all the way to the bottom of the mat. You will see all the dirt and soap run out of the mat. Keep doing this until all the dirt and soap is completely gone. Hang the mats to dry. It's a good idea to do this before washing the car so that they can be drying all day while you're doing the detail.

De-grease the Engine

If you are going to offer your customers engine cleaning, you need a pressure washer. A pressure washer produces enough force to remove the dirt and grease from the engine.

CAUTION! Volvo's can be very sensitive to engine cleaning. I rarely had any problems with BMW, Mercedes, Lexus, Toyota, Honda, Audi or big trucks like Chevy, Ford or Dodge just to name a few off the top of my head. If a car doesn't start after cleaning, water may have gotten into the distributor. Try blowing it out with the air compressor. Most newer cars have plastic covers to protect the sensitive electronic parts of the engine.

Stand at the front of the car with the engine cool and dry. Start by spraying de-greaser onto the underside of the hood if needed. Then spray de-greaser on the engine, thoroughly covering everything you can see from the front, then move to each side of the engine and cover everything you can see from each side. This way you hit every angle. Be careful not to let the de-greaser drip down onto the paint. Once the entire engine compartment is covered, let the de-greaser soak. You will rinse with the pressure washer after the wheels and tires are cleaned.

Tip: If you're worried about getting de-greaser on the paint, just wet the two front quarter panels down. Then, if it does drip, it won't stain the paint.

De-grease the Wheel Wells and Door Jambs

Spray degreaser in all the wheel wells and door jambs (including the trunk door jambs).

Let the degreaser soak. You will rinse with the pressure washer after the wheels and tires are cleaned.

Clean the Wheels and Tires

Dilute the wheel cleaner as per the directions. Do one wheel at a time. Never spray wheel acid on all four wheels and just let it soak.

Always start with a cool surface. For chrome or clear-coated wheels it's usually ok to use an acid based wheel cleaner. Always test on a small inconspicuous area of the wheel to make sure you don't get a reaction from the product. If it foams up and turns white, immediately rinse it, then clean it using an acid-free wheel cleaner (always test first). For polished or anodized aluminum wheels use an acid-free wheel cleaner.

WARNING! *Acid can be damaging if left on too long. Always wear gloves and protective eye wear! Never use acid on aluminum! This will stain and etch the finish.*

Once you have determined which type of cleaner to use, spray one wheel and use a spoke brush to agitate the dirt. Rinse with water. Next, spray degreaser on the wall of the tire and brush with a white wall tire brush. Rinse well with cool water. Go on to the next wheel until all four are clean. Sometimes it's good to pressure wash during your final rinse. Rinse wheels until water runs clean.

Tip: If you can't get to all parts of the wheel, rotate the wheels 1/2 a turn by pulling the car forward.

Rinse the Engine, Wheel Wells, Door Jambs and the Car

CAUTION! *When using a pressure washer to wash the car, be very careful not to hold the wand too close or you could damage the paint. Start at 2 feet away. You'll get a feel for how close you can safely get. Be especially careful around recently re-painted areas, moldings and pin stripes, those areas are very sensitive to pressure washing.*

Use the pressure washer to rinse. Start with the underside of the hood, then the engine from the front and then each side. Be gentle around distributer cap, but spray everywhere deep inside. It may seem like overkill but if you don't do it this way, later on when you pop the hood to dress, you will see all the spots you missed and you'll wish you had listened to me. Close the hood and rinse the entire car, rinsing the wheel wells and door jambs as you move around the car.

Removing Stickers

Note: Always check with the owner before removing stickers, they may not want them removed.

Most stickers can be safely removed from the outside glass and painted surfaces using the pressure washer during the wash. To remove the more stubborn stickers from glass all you need is a razor blade and some glass cleaner. Spray the glass cleaner onto the sticker and let it soak in. Then use the razor blade to lift the edges and peel back the sticker. Remove any left over adhesive with the glass cleaner and razor blade.

Removing stickers from the painted parts is a little more difficult. If you are not able to get them off safely with the pressure washer during the wash, the best way to remove these is to heat them up with a heat gun. Once heated, they will usually peel right off. Use the DX330 to remove the adhesive that's left over. DO NOT try and remove the stickers with the razor blade. You will cut in to the paint.

Wash the Car

Wash the car, starting with the tops and working your way down. It's best to wash in the shade so you don't get water spots. If you have to wash in the sun, it's a good idea to wash and rinse in sections so that the soap doesn't dry out on the car.

Use the bug sponge on the front grill area, the back of the side mirrors, the windshield and anywhere else that may have bug residue.

Rinse the car. You can either hose it off or use the pressure washer.

Dry the car with a chamois.

Open the doors and clean all the door jambs and weather stripping with a chamois or a towel. If you do a thorough job here, it will save you a lot of time later on. These areas are much easier to clean while they are still wet. (Don't forget the trunk jamb).

Dress the Engine

WARNING! *Only use water based products for dressing the engine area. Silicone products could catch fire when the engine is hot.*

Use the air compressor to blow the excess water out of the engine and engine compartment. Blow all the engine hoses and parts deep down inside. Spray dressing on the engine, thoroughly covering everything you can see from the front, then move to each side of the engine and cover everything you can see from each side. After the dressing has covered the engine, shut the hood and continue with the rest of the detail. You will wipe it all down later, after the dressing has time to soak in.

Interior Detail System

I believe this system is the fastest and the most efficient way to do an interior detail. We did the interiors this way because this system works well when you have several cars to do each day. Basically, the whole idea when doing an interior detail is to clean every inch of the interior from headliner down to the foot pedals and everywhere in between. Evaluate the interior to determine what needs to be done to get it clean. If it's not very dirty, you don't have to spend a lot of time scrubbing. Some cars just need to be wiped down with interior cleaner and spot cleaned with a brush and soapy water; other cars need every inch to be scrubbed. For example: A smoker's car will probably need to be scrubbed down from top to bottom.

Interior Prep

Use the air compressor to blow out any hard to reach spaces like between the seats, under the seats, vents, pockets on doors. On SUV's and hatchbacks that have folding back seats be sure to flip the seats up so you can clean underneath them. Minivans have removable backs seats. Removing the seats will make it much easier to clean. When you are done blowing, do a quick vacuum. You will do a final vacuum when you're all done cleaning the interior.

In a bucket, mix interior shampoo with warm water. Put your scrub brushes in the bucket.

Let's start at the driver side. In this case the sections should be cleaned in the following order:

- ✓ Section 1 - Front, Driver Side
- ✓ Section 2 - Rear, Driver Side.
- ✓ Section 3 - Trunk or Cargo Area
- ✓ Section 4 - Rear, Passenger Side.
- ✓ Section 5 - Front, Passenger Side.

Start in section 1 and do steps 1-3 before moving to the next section. Work around the car like clock work. This system breaks the interior up into 5 parts. If you follow this system you won't be running around in circles.

Following this order makes it easier to move all the equipment from one section to the next, because you are only moving a short distance around the car.

Tip: When you are working on the front sections, roll the seat all the way back. When you are working in the back sections, roll the seat all the way forward.

Step 1 - Clean the Carpet

Spray the carpet with spot cleaner where needed. Use the soapy brush and thoroughly scrub the carpet. Go over the carpet with a clean, dry towel. You should see the dirt come up in the towel. If the carpet is very dirty, use the extractor. Spray with the trigger and work the wand back and forth, and then suck all the water and dirt out. When using the extractor always suck up as much of the water as you can. After using the extractor, go over the carpet with a clean dry towel. Be sure to clean the little patch of carpet on the door.

If you come across any stubborn stains like oil, grease, ink marks, lipstick, crayon marks or smoke film you might try Awesome Orange (Pro®). It does a great job and it's environmentally safe. If you ever come across gum, tar or felt pen stains, try the California Orange (Pro®).

When working in the drivers section, clean the foot pedals with Dow Cleaner and the air compressor.

WARNING! Never spray or wipe any kind of dressing on the foot pedals as this will cause them to be slippery.

When you are done cleaning the carpet, move on to step 2.

Step 2 - Clean the Leather, Vinyl, Rubber and Plastic

CAUTION! Always test an area first before you just dive right in. Sometimes different cleaners or chemicals can stain leather or different materials.

The best cleaner I have found for cleaning the majority of the interior is Dow Cleaner (Scrubbing Bubbles). You can use it to clean plastic, rubber and vinyl. Using Dow Cleaner with the air compressor forces the dirt out of the nooks and cracks that are hard to get to with a brush. Spray the Dow cleaner, wipe dry, and then blow with the air compressor. Wipe again so you don't leave any residue.

WARNING! Never leave Dow Cleaner on a surface for too long as it may cause staining.

When you open the door the first thing you notice is the bottom part of the door jamb, it is a long plastic part that runs down the length of the jamb. Sometimes after you scrub it, there are still scuff marks. To get the scuff marks out take a little piece of steel wool and Dow cleaner and rub it gently over the scuff marks. They should come right off.

Spray Dow Cleaner on a towel and clean the door jamb and rubber weather stripping.

Spray interior cleaner on a towel and clean the door panels or, if it's very dirty, scrub lightly with a soft nylon brush and soapy water. Clean all areas on and around the door.

Use Dow Cleaner and the air compressor to clean the door handle and all the buttons on the handle then wipe dry with a towel. If these areas are not very dirty, you may just want to spray some interior cleaner on a towel and wipe.

Check the headliner. If dirty, spray your interior cleaner onto a towel then wipe the headliner. You never want to get the headliner very wet because the glue could start to loosen up and then it will sag.

Additional steps when working in the front seat sections

- Clean the dashboard and the instrument panel.

- Clean the steering wheel. It's ok to scrub the steering wheel with the nylon brush if needed. Clean all the levers, switches and buttons around the steering wheel.

- Clean and blow in between the seats, clean the center console area and the cup holders.

- Check the ash tray. If it's very dirty, soak it in soapy water then lightly scrub with a brush and towel dry.

- Spray Dow cleaner on the vents, wipe with a towel then blow with the air compressor. This gives them a clean dressed look.

- Clean the visor, front and back. Clean the glove box inside and out.

Additional steps when working in the rear seat sections

- Clean all the plastic parts on the bottom of the front seat with Dow cleaner and the air compressor. If this area is not very dirty you may only need to do a quick wipe with interior cleaner, but be sure to clean everything.

- Clean the back and the sides of the center console area.

Step 3 - Clean the Seat

Tip: By cleaning the seat last you never have to sit on a wet seat!

Adjust the seat to the reclined position so that you can clean all of it. When cleaning the seat, start at the head rest then work your way down. Clean the sides then the bottom part and don't forget the arm rest. When cleaning the back seat be sure to open up the big arm rest that sits in the middle. Blow it out and clean the top, bottom and all sides. On SUV's and hatchbacks that have folding back seats, flip the seats up so you can clean the sides and underneath. Be sure to clean the seat belts and buckles. Pro® has a product called Seatbelt Cleaner and Spot Removal. You will clean the back side of the front seats when you are working in the rear sections.

Fabric Seats

If the seat is made of fabric and it's very dirty, you will need to use the extractor. Spray spot cleaner on a section of the seat and agitate the dirt with a soapy brush. Now use the extractor, spraying with the trigger and, then sucking all the water and dirt out. Do this a section at a time until the entire seat is clean. When using the extractor always suck up as much of the water as you can. After using the extractor, go over the seat with a clean dry towel. You never want to leave the interior very wet. If spray gets on your clean center console area, just wipe it up when you're done extracting.

Leather Seats

Be careful when working with leather seats. Some products can cause staining or strip the finish. If they are very dirty just lightly brush with interior soap and water then wipe dry. Lexol makes products especially for cleaning and conditioning leather.

Vinyl Seats

Vinyl seats are pretty easy to clean. You can spray Dow Cleaner and brush lightly then wipe. Do small sections at a time. Don't let product sit on vinyl for a long time. It could cause staining.

Once you are done with the seat, move on to the next section and go back to step 1.

Clean the Trunk (Section 3)

Remove everything from the trunk and vacuum. If there are any greasy spots on the carpet, spray the area with degreaser and scrub with a nylon brush. Go over the area with a dry towel. Sometimes you might have to use the extractor. Don't forget to vacuum and clean around the spare tire area. You might have to remove the tire first. Clean and dress the weather stripping with the interior dressing if needed. Wipe the sides of the trunk down with the Dow cleaner or interior cleaner. It's up to you if you want to dress the trunk area. Place everything back into the trunk when you're finished.

Dress the Interior

Spray interior dressing onto a clean towel and dress all of the vinyl, rubber and plastic in each section. Don't ever spray the interior dressing directly onto the surface. You can spray the vents and other hard to reach places with the spray dressing and then wipe with the towel. Just remember to blend and never leave it greasy. You don't want anything wet, running or drooling. You just want everything to look clean and blended.

Tip: After cleaning the interior, always leave the windows down a few inches so the interior can get lots of air. If you leave it all closed up, the windows will steam up and the interior will start to smell bad.

Exterior Detail System

Remove Road Tar

Road tar tends to build up on the lower panels behind each wheel and on the painted inside edge of the wheel wells. To remove the tar spray the area with DX330, wait a minute to let the product work, then wipe with a towel. You can find DX330 at an automotive paint store. Always wear gloves when using this product!

Clay the Car

Using clay is the best way to remove contaminants like fall-out, acid rain, rail dust and overspray from the surface of the paint. There are two types of clay. One is very aggressive and is used for over-spray, rail dust and fall-out removal. The other clay is mild and is used for cars that don't have heavy duty contaminants on it. You should always polish or wax after you use clay because it removes the wax and it will leave a residue on the finish.

Evaluate the painted surfaces to determine which type of clay to use. The most common problem areas are the top surfaces. If you start with the mild clay and it's not doing the job, switch to the more aggressive clay. Clay is always used with a water based lubricant. Paint gloss is a good product to use.

Always start with a cool, clean surface. Use about 1/3 of the clay bar at a time. You will start at one side and work your way around the car, from the front to the rear, then from the rear to the front on the other side.

Work on about a 2' x 2' area at a time. Spray the area with paint gloss, and then rub the clay back and forth over the lubricated area along the lines of the car until smooth. Wipe the completed area with a damp chamois. When you can see the fall-out and rail dust on the clay, knead the clay to get a fresh surface.

Using the High Speed Buffer

Anyone wanting to learn how to detail cars and run their own professional detail shop needs to learn how to use a high speed buffer. I would recommend anyone who is serious about detailing should consider working for a dealership or a detail shop to get some hands on experience. If you don't have any training you could cause damage to a car. Some Pro® distributors offer hands on training. They will come to your shop and show you and your employees the proper way to use the buffer. I highly recommend this. They will even send you and your employees a "certificate of completion" that you can frame and hang up on your wall.

Before you begin cutting you should determine whether the vehicle has a clear coat. Around 95% of all cars being manufactured right now have been painted using a base coat/clear coat system. This system consists of one or more layers of primer, a color layer and a clear top layer. The color layer is usually very thin. The clear coat can be two to three times the thickness of the color layer and adds depth and gloss to the finish. If you are not sure whether a vehicle has a clear coat you can determine this by hand applying a compound to an inconspicuous area of the paint. If no color appears on the rag it has a clear coat.

Evaluate the condition of the paint to determine what products to use. There are different stages of cut from mild to very aggressive. These products remove a micro-layer of clear coat in order to remove light scratches and oxidation. Experienced detailers will know exactly what to use on a car just by looking at it. You want to be aggressive enough to remove any oxidation and scratches but not any more aggressive than needed.

If there aren't a lot of surface scratches and oxidation in the finish and you are looking for that deep shine, just give it a good polish then apply wax or paint sealant.

If the paint is in extremely poor condition with heavy oxidation and scratches you will have to use a white wool cutting pad with heavy duty compound, and then follow up with your foam cutting pad and a milder cut, then polish and wax. In most cases you will do what is called a 3 step (cut, polish, wax). When you use compound you will put swirls in the finish but don't worry, you will remove them when you polish.

Let's take a black car that is four years old and has light scratches and moderate oxidation. I would say you should start with a medium compound. Most detailers have their favorite products. Also, some detailers have experimented with mixing products. The cut that I used on a daily basis was a mixture of 2/3 Duz-All (PRO®) and 1/3 3M Perfect-It lll rubbing compound. If I needed a more aggressive cut, I would add more Perfect-It or use the Perfect-It alone. If you decide you want to try mixing these two products make sure to mix them well.

You can find 3M Perfect-IT lll rubbing compound at an automotive paint store. It's very effective, easy to use and easy to clean up. I believe it's the very best compound out there.

Duz-All (PRO®) is a clear coat cleaner that is safe on all finishes, base coat and clear coat. You can use it by hand or by machine.

Step 1 – Cut

If the car is a convertible, put the top down to prevent product from splattering onto the material. Cover up the windshield wiper blades with sleeves or wrap them with towels. It helps with the clean up later. Use a yellow waffle foam pad. I like the waffle foam pad from PRO® that's 1 1/2 inches thick. It's very soft and easy to use.

Tip: Always apply product closer to the middle of the panel so that it doesn't ooze down into the cracks.

Standing at the side of the hood, choose a 2' x 2' section of the hood and apply a small amount of compound (about the size of a quarter). Some detailers have a bad habit of applying the product in a line. The problem is, once you set the buffer down on that line and start the buffer, the product splatters all over.

Take the cord and place it over your shoulder. Stand up straight with knees bent a little and place the buffer right on top of the product. Gently squeeze the trigger and spread the product around the section you are going to buff. Now begin buffing the area keeping the speed 1200-1800 rpm. Keeping the buffer between your shoulder blades and keeping the pad as flat as possible on the painted surface, move the buffer in straight lines slowly to the left then slowly to the right. Buff in about a 2' x 2' section. You never need to buff over 1800 rpm. If you are new at using a high speed buffer I would suggest starting at the lower speed of 1000 rpm until you get a feel for it. It's important to stay within the shoulder blades because when you stretch and turn your body to the sides it's hard to keep your movements in straight lines and keep even pressure on the pad. Remember, you will put swirls in during the cutting process. You want the swirls to be in uniform straight lines so that they will be easier to remove during the polishing process.

When the product is all worked in, stop buffing and move over to the next section of the hood. Apply more compound and start the process again. You might have to divide 1/2 the hood up to 4 - 6 parts. Be sure to connect where you left off to where you began.

Work your way around the car, from the front to the rear, then from the rear to the front on the other side. Clean your pad regularly with a foam pad cleaning tool or blow it out it with the air.

When working on the roof top, be careful coming down that back quarter panel area. Don't burn the moldings. If you are worried about burning the edges and the moldings you can tape all those areas up with masking tape. It takes a little more time, but you don't have to worry if you happen to hit the edge.

When buffing the sides of the car, bend your knees into a squatting position so that you stay at eye level with the buffer.

Don't forget to buff out the side mirrors. You can even buff plastic side mirrors if needed to remove oxidation. Always turn your buffer down low while doing these small areas.

Step 2 – Polish

Tip: I always used two different polishing pads. One was black and I only used it on dark color cars. The other was a lighter color and I used that one for light color cars. That way I wouldn't mix the products on the pads.

Polishing removes the swirls that you put in when cutting and brings back the shine in the finish. For a black car you might consider using a product called Sleek, a cleaner glaze made by Car Brite. You only need a small amount of this product with a black polishing pad. It brings out the deep rich shine that black cars deserve to have. It also helps remove swirls and compound scratches. To polish a car you need to use the same technique as cutting. Like I said before, it's important not to turn your body to the sides. Keep the buffer speed in between 1200-1800 rpm and stay with in a 2' x 2' area. Be sure to clean your pad with the cleaning tool often. You can polish the tail light covers and the headlight covers if you can get your buffer in there. Don't forget to polish out the side mirrors!

Once you have completed polishing, look for any painted areas that could not be reached with the buffer that might need some attention. One common problem area is under the door handles. This area gets little scratches from finger nails. On a light colored car these scratches really stand out because the scratches collect dirt. The best way to fix this is to use a clear coat cleaner like Duz-All on an applicator pad and rub the area out by hand.

Step 3 – Apply Wax or Sealant

The final step is all about protecting the paint. If you are applying a wax, you can apply it by hand with an applicator pad or use an orbital. If you are applying sealant, always use an orbital. For the best results, use a GEM orbital polisher. The Gem is great for removing swirls from dark colored cars.

Using the Gem Orbital Polisher

Place the orbital on the ground or table with the bonnet facing up. Dampen the bonnet's surface by misting it with water. Spin the top and squeeze a line of product (wax or sealant) starting from the center out to the edge. Place the orbital on the side of the hood you're going to work on first. Place the cord over your shoulder and hold onto the handles. Once you are ready, turn on the switch and guide the orbital from side to side. This orbital is heavy so let the orbital do the work. Once the product dries to a haze, move on to the next section. When you want to stop, be sure to keep the orbital flat on the surface of the car and turn off the switch. Never pick the orbital up off the surface while spinning. Always turn it off first, let it come to a complete stop, and then pick it up.

You can also remove the product from the paint using this orbital. Just place a soft microfiber towel onto the car surface then place the orbital on top of the towel start the orbital and guide it around the car.

Using the Porter Cable Orbital

This orbital is small, lightweight and easy to use. Place a finishing pad on the Velcro backing plate. Try to get it on as straight as possible. Put the product onto the pad and set the orbital onto the surface. Turn it on and guide it from side to side. With this orbital you can work the product in to the paint by guiding it back and forth until you see the product starts disappearing.

Finishing Up

Tip: It's a good idea to apply the exterior dressing before removing the wax or sealant. That way, if you get dressing on the paint, it will be removed along with the wax.

Apply Bumper Kote® (Car Brite) to a foam applicator and spread evenly over the bumpers and trim. Use the spray dressing to dress any hard to reach places like the front grill area. Try not to get dressing on the paint.

Working on one wheel at a time, spray the wheel well with tire dressing, covering everywhere you can see. Take a 3" paint brush and dip it into the tire dressing. Brush the dressing evenly onto the walls of the tires. Wipe down the wheels using window cleaner for chrome wheels or paint gloss for clear coated wheels. You might need to pull the car forward to dress the bottom part of the tire.

Remove the wax or sealant with a clean soft microfiber towel. The product should come off easily. Don't rub very hard, that could cause scratching. When removing the product start at one end of the car and work your way around the car until all product is removed.

Wipe all the bumpers, trim and tires to remove any excess dressing. Never leave the trim gooey. If you leave a lot of excess dressing on the tires, it will fly all over the sides of the car when the customer drives away.

Open the hood, trunk and doors to remove any wax or dust from buffing that may have accumulated in the cracks.

Wipe down the engine compartment if needed.

Shine any chrome with #0000 steel wool and Sprayway glass cleaner. Always test a small area when using steel wool to make sure it's not scratching the finish. Don't forget the hood emblem, tailpipes and running boards.

Most luxury cars have chrome and wood trim throughout the interior. If cleaned with the Dow cleaner they will look smudgy. Clean these areas with Sprayway window cleaner. Spray the window cleaner onto the towel so that you don't get it on the dressed areas. If the chrome needs to be shined up, use the steel wool, it does a great job. Be careful not to scratch the leather while cleaning the chrome with the steel wool. Check for chrome inside the door jambs.

Clean the windows and mirrors inside and out. Use the Sprayway window cleaner. Use one towel for cleaning and one for drying. Make sure the towels are clean and don't have any residue on them. Roll all the windows down a few inches and clean all top edges. Now roll the windows up. Clean the outside of the windows and the side mirror on the driver's side. Then clean the inside of the windows and the inside mirrors. Repeat the process on the passenger side. If the car has a sunroof window make sure you clean that too.

Now do your final dust and vacuum. Use a small soft brush to dust the dashboard, console, instrument panel and all the vents. Vacuum the carpets and seats. Be sure to get in between the seats. Roll the seats back when you are working in the front seat sections and roll the seats forward when you are working the back seat sections. Vacuum the rear window area. If it's an SUV or hatchback, be sure to flip the back seats up and vacuum underneath. When you are all done there should not be any dust anywhere and the interior should look perfect. Vacuum the mats and place them back in the car.

If the car is a convertible, vacuum the top.

When the detail is complete, it's very important to take the car outside into the natural light to check the windows for streaks and smudges. Also, check the exterior for sealant or wax you might have missed. Use a detail brush and remove any product that might have gotten into cracks or around the moldings.

CHAPTER

Additional Services

Wash and Wax

You can offer a Wash and Wax as a maintenance service between details.

Clean the Wheels and Tires

WARNING! Never use acid on aluminum! This will stain and etch the finish.

Wash the Car

CAUTION! When using a pressure washer to wash the car, be very careful not to hold the wand too close or you could damage the paint. Start at 2 feet away. You'll get a feel for how close you can safely get. Be especially careful around recently re-painted areas. Also, be careful when using the pressure washer around moldings and pin stripes, those areas are very sensitive to pressure washing.

- Rinse the car with cool water.

- Wash the car, starting with the top and working your way down.

- Use the bug sponge on the front grill area, the back of the side mirrors, the windshield and anywhere else that has bug residue.

- Rinse with cool water.

- Dry the car with a chamois.

- Open the doors and wipe down all the door jambs with the chamois. (Don't forget the trunk).

- Remove road tar from the lower panels if needed.

Apply Wax

You can apply wax by hand with an applicator pad or use an orbital. To apply it by hand, dampen the applicator pad, apply a small amount of wax about the size of a quarter onto the pad then starting toward the middle of a panel apply the wax in circular motions in a very thin layer. You want to avoid getting wax into the cracks or onto the trim.

Finishing Up

- Dress the tires and the wheel wells.

- Dress the exterior trim if needed

- Remove the wax with a soft microfiber towel.

- Clean the chrome if needed.

- Wipe down the wheels and make sure there isn't any brake dust anywhere on the rims.

- Wipe down the dash area.

- If you notice anything in the interior that you can clean up quickly and easily like coffee stains in the cup holders or maybe a small spot on the carpet, a nice thing to do is to clean it. If you take this extra step your customers will really appreciate it.

- Use a small soft brush to dust the dashboard, console, instrument panel and all the vents.

- Be sure to check the ash trays, the pockets on the doors and the pockets on the back seats for trash.

- Clean the windows and mirrors inside and out.

- Vacuum the rear window area.

- After you have finished be sure to roll the car outside into the natural light and check for any streaks and smudges.

New Car Protection Package

This service includes a paint sealant application, interior fabric guard application and leather conditioning. Since the car is new, it doesn't take as much time as a complete detail but you can price this service at about the same price or more. Make sure to list this service in your yellow page ad. The dealerships will often tell people that paint sealant lasts 5 years. They charge up to $1200 for the sealant application. What most dealerships don't tell them is that they will need to have the sealant re-applied within the first year and if they don't bring it in for re-application, it falls out of warrantee. We would charge up to $350 for this service and give our customers a year warrantee.

Below are the steps for doing a new car protection package.

- ✓ Clean the wheels and tires
- ✓ Wash the car
- ✓ Wipe all door jambs (Don't forget trunk jambs)
- ✓ Dust and vacuum the interior and trunk area
- ✓ Spray Fabric guard on all floor mats, seats and carpets
- ✓ If leather, condition leather seats and doors
- ✓ Clay car then apply paint sealant with the orbital
- ✓ Dress tires, wheel wells and all the trim
- ✓ Take off paint sealant
- ✓ Clean and shine chrome
- ✓ Clean windows inside and out.

WARNING! Do not spray fabric guard on leather or vinyl. It will stain!

<u>Interior Detail</u>

Occasionally a customer will want only the interior to be cleaned. Some of the steps are different than those of a Complete Detail, so we have included a checklist for the Interior Detail.

Wash the Car

When doing only an interior detail I suggest first doing a quick exterior wash. Most detailers would say "their only paying for the interior why wash it?" Well first of all, it's a nice thing to do and your customers will appreciate it. Second, you will probably need to degrease the door jambs and trunk jambs, so you are getting it wet anyway. I say, "Just wash it!"

- ✓ Pressure wash the floor mats
- ✓ Clean the wheels and tires
- ✓ De-grease all door jambs including the trunk
- ✓ Rinse car with cool water
- ✓ Wash the car
- ✓ Chamois dry
- ✓ Wipe all door jambs and trunk jamb

Interior Prep

Use the air compressor to blow out any hard to reach spaces

Interior Detail System

Start in section 1 and do steps 1-3 before moving to the next section. Work around the car like clock work. This system breaks the interior up into 5 parts. If you follow this system you won't be running around in circles. Let's start at the driver side. In this case the sections should be cleaned in the following order:

- ✓ Section 1 - Front, Driver Side
- ✓ Section 2 - Rear, Driver Side.
- ✓ Section 3 - Trunk or Cargo Area
- ✓ Section 4 - Rear, Passenger Side.
- ✓ Section 5 - Front, Passenger Side.

Following this order makes it easier to move all the equipment from one section to the next, because you are only moving a short distance around the car.

Tip: When you are working on the front sections, roll the seat all the way back. When you are working in the back sections, roll the seat all the way forward.

In a bucket, mix interior shampoo with warm water. Put your scrub brushes in the bucket.

- ✓ Step 1 - Clean the Carpet
- ✓ Step 2 - Clean the Leather, Vinyl, Rubber and Plastic
- ✓ Step 3 - Clean the Seat
- ✓ Clean the Trunk (Section 3)

Finishing up

- ✓ Dress the interior
- ✓ Clean the interior chrome and wood trim
- ✓ Clean the windows and mirrors inside and out
- ✓ Final dust and vacuum
- ✓ Vacuum the mats and put them back in.
- ✓ Dress the tires, wheel wells
- ✓ Take the car outside in the natural light to check for streaks and smudges.

Tip: After cleaning the interior, always leave the windows down a few inches so the interior can get lots of air. If you leave it all closed up, the windows will steam up and the interior will start to smell bad.

Exterior Detail

Occasionally a customer will want only the exterior to be polished and waxed. Some of the steps are different than those of a Complete Detail, so we have included a checklist for the Exterior Detail.

Wash the Car

- ✓ Clean the wheels and tires
- ✓ Rinse the car with the pressure washer.
- ✓ Wash the car
- ✓ Rinse the car
- ✓ Dry the car with a chamois.
- ✓ Wipe down all the door jambs

Exterior Detail System

- ✓ Remove road tar
- ✓ Clay the car
- ✓ Cut if needed
- ✓ Polish
- ✓ Apply wax or sealant

Finishing Up

✓ Dress the bumpers and trim

✓ Dress the wheel wells and tires

✓ Remove the wax or sealant

✓ Remove any excess dressing from bumpers, trim and tires

✓ Open the hood, trunk and doors to remove any wax or dust

✓ Shine the chrome

✓ Clean the windows and mirrors inside and out

✓ Final dust and vacuum

✓ If the car is a convertible, vacuum the top

It's very important to take the car outside in the natural light to check the windows for streaks and smudges. Also, check the exterior for sealant or wax you might have missed. Use a detail brush and remove any product that might have gotten into cracks or around the moldings.

Cleaning and Protecting Convertible Tops

Vinyl

To clean a convertible top that's made of vinyl, wash with the car wash soap and a wash mitt. If it's really dirty you can use a soft nylon brush and scrub it down gently. Rinse well. Dry with a chamois.

303 Aerospace Protectant is a great product for conditioning and protecting vinyl tops after cleaning. Spray the product onto a soft cloth and rub it into the vinyl top. Work your way around the top until it's all covered and blended.

Cloth

You can find these tops on Mercedes and other luxury cars. Wash with the wash mitt and interior shampoo. Spot clean if needed. Do not use any heavy duty cleaners or degreasers on this top. Be sure to rinse very well. It's made of cloth, so it's going to take a little longer to rinse. Dry the top with a chamois. Vacuum the top with the Shop Vac.

303 High Tech Fabric Guard is a great product for protecting cloth convertible tops. The surface should be clean and

completely dry. Before application, mask all the windows and painted parts adjacent to the edges of the top to prevent overspray. You are more likely to get an even coating if you apply two lighter coats rather than one heavy coat. Let the first coating dry to the touch before applying the second coat. You should definitely charge extra for this service as it takes additional time and materials.

Cleaning Plastic Rear Windows

Many convertible tops have a plastic rear window. If not treated, they can start to yellow and then fall apart. 3M makes a good plastic cleaner and polish. You should start with the cleaner and follow it up with the polish. The inside of the window can be more difficult to clean since it is usually in a confined space. You don't want to get any product on the vinyl or cloth as it could stain so always mask the edges of the top around the window when using these products. You should charge extra for this service since it takes extra work and time.

<u>Wet-Sanding</u>

Wet-sanding is a method to get rid of surface scratches or etching from bird droppings that are too deep to be buffed out. It is also the only way to get rid of "orange peel". The wet sanding process actually resurfaces the clear coat and is more aggressive than compound. Extreme care must be taken not to sand through the clear coat.

WARNING! *You can burn the paint if you sand too deep. This technique is for more advanced detailers.*

Evaluate the scratches. If you can feel the scratch with your finger nail it could be too deep to remove completely. You may be able to partially remove these deeper scratches but you can't completely remove them because you would have to sand to deep into the clear-coat. Partially removing the scratch can still improve the appearance but you should let your customer know what to expect.

Surface scratches look a lot like scrapes or scuffs. Look at the scratches from the side to see if you notice any dents. If there are, let your customer know and price out the scratch removal and the PDR work.

To remove scratches or etching use 2000 grit sandpaper. The scratches from this paper will be fairly easy to remove by buffing with compound and a white wool pad.

Wet Sanding Process

- Soak your sand paper in a bucket of water for at least 30 minutes. This softens up the paper. Wrap the paper around a soft foam backing block. Using the block will give you a more evenly sanded surface than you can get using your fingers.

- Use a spray bottle of water to wet the area to be sanded.

- Sand the damaged area with very light pressure using a back and forth motion. Be sure to sand in the same direction over the entire area you are working on. Keep the area and the paper wet at all times. You can check your work by wiping the area with a chamois and drying with the air compressor. The sanded area will have a whitish appearance, don't worry this is normal. You might have to repeat this process several times until the scratches are removed.

- If you're wet-sanding on a side panel, the wet-sanding run-off will run down the panel. If there are any moldings below the sanding area, it's a good idea to wipe the run-off with a chamois because bits of debris in the run-off can get lodged in the crevices.

- When you're done sanding, use a wool pad and compound to remove the sanding scratches. Follow up with a foam cutting pad and some Perfect It lII rubbing compound then use a polishing pad with some 3M Finesse or a polish.

- Apply wax using an orbital. You must always cut, polish and wax after wet-sanding. If you try and cut corners here, you will be able to see the scratches from the sanding process.

Water Spot Removal

Water spots are caused by hard water, usually from a sprinkler, which has been allowed to evaporate on the cars surface. This leaves behind minerals that can damage the paint. The most effective way to remove water spots from the paint finish, windows and chrome is an acid wash.

WARNING! *Acid can be damaging if left on too long. Acid washing should only be done in the shade on a cool, clean surface. Always wear gloves and protective eye wear! Never use acid on aluminum! This will stain and etch the finish.*

- First, wash the car with car wash soap and rinse as usual.

- Pour un-diluted wheel acid on a rag or sponge then wipe it onto the area that has the water spots. Do a small section at a time. You will feel the acid breaking up the mineral deposits. Let the acid work for 30 seconds then rinse the area thoroughly with cool water.

- Repeat the process until the water spots are gone. It is very important to rinse often since the acid can damage the finish if it's left on too long.

- Finish up with a polish and wax

Glossary

Abrasives: Used in compounds and polishes to remove oxidation and smooth the edges of fine scratches and swirl marks, reducing or removing their appearance.

Basecoat: The pigmented color coat of paint that gives the vehicle its color.

Base coat/Clear coat System: A two-stage finish consisting of a color coat and a clear coat.

Body Filler: Material used to fill dents in damaged auto body parts.

Buffing: Using a high speed buffer and polish to bring out gloss and/or remove scratches and oxidation.

Burn/Burn Through: Polishing or buffing of a color or clear coat too hard or too long causing the underlying coat(s) to be revealed.

Carnauba: Obtained from the leaves of the carnauba palm, carnauba in its purest form is very hard and brittle. Carnauba

Glossary

goes through a process of being mixed with petroleum solvents to soften it so that it can be easily applied as paint protection.

Clay: Used to remove contaminants such as paint overspray and rail dust from the finish.

Cleaner: A very mild polish which relies primarily on chemical cleaners (solvents) to clean the finish.

Cleaner-wax: A very mild polish which contains wax.

Clear Coat: A clear paint usually made of polyurethane. Clear Coat is applied as a second coat over a base coat of pigmented paint in two-stage paint finishes, commonly referred to as base coat/clear coat finishes. Though Clear Coat contains UV inhibitors, it is not maintenance-free and does degrade like pigmented paint due to UV rays and acid rain. Therefore it needs to be polished and waxed/sealed on a regular basis to maintain depth and gloss.

Compound: A highly abrasive form of polish also known as "cut" used primarily to remove heavy oxidation and surface scratches from the paint finish.

Glossary

E.P.A. (Environmental Protection Agency): Government agency established to administer federal environmental legislation.

Fading: A gradual change of color or gloss in a finish.

Fisheyes: Round ring-like craters in the paint finish caused by contamination

Glaze: A very fine polishing material used to gain gloss and shine.

Gloss: Reflectance of light from a painted surface.

Masking: Process of applying pressure sensitive tape and paper to a vehicle to prevent paint from being applied where it is not wanted.

Microfiber: A fiber consisting of polyester fibers that are finer than hair or silk. Microfiber towels, will not scratch the paint finish, are resistant to oils and chemicals, and wash very easily.

Orange Peel: Texture in a paint finish that resembles the peel of an orange; caused by improper reduction or application.

Glossary

Oxidation:
Chemical reaction between oxygen and another substance, causing paint film curing, paint film failure or metal rusting.

Ozone Oder Remover: An air purification device that removes odors.

Paint Chips: Small chips in the finish usually due to the impact of rocks and stones.

Paint Over-spray: Paint which, during application, adheres to panels not intended to be painted.

Paint Sealant: A synthetic paint protection that contains polymers that bond to the finish for longer lasting protection.

Paintless Dent Repair (PDR): A technique that removes door dings and hail damage without the need for sanding, body filler or repainting.

Glossary

Polish: A product that contains abrasives to smooth paint and remove oxidation. Also contains conditioners and oils to enhance gloss and depth.

Refinish: The act of replacing or repairing a painted surface.

Silicone: Used in polishes and waxes to make application and removal easy. Also enhances gloss, water-resistance, and durability.

Single-stage Paint: Consists of two coats of colored paint and does not have a clear-coat applied.

Solvent Cleaner: Solvent-based cleaning product used to remove contamination from surfaces prior to polishing.

Swirl Mark: A circular scratch in the paint finish usually caused by the use of a machine buffer or a dirty wash mitt.

Wax: A product that is applied to protect the paint finish.

CPSIA information can be obtained
at www.ICGtesting.com
Printed in the USA
FFOW01n1336301115
19137FF

9 780615 226873